Department of Education and Science

Classics
from 5 to 16

Curriculum Matters 12
AN HMI SERIES

LONDON · HER MAJESTY'S STATIONERY OFFICE

ISBN 0 11 270663 0

Contents

	Page
Preface	iv
Introduction	1
The nature and scope of the subject	2
The aims of classics teaching	4
Classical civilisation	5
Objectives in the primary and early secondary years	5
Planning and organisation in the primary and early secondary years	10
Objectives in GCSE-related work	14
Planning and organisation of GCSE-related work	16
Principles of teaching and learning	18
Classical languages	20
Context	20
Objectives in the early stages	22
Objectives at the GCSE stage	26
Principles of teaching and learning	29
Differentiation	33
Assessment	36
Conclusion	39

Preface

Since 1984 HM Inspectorate has published a number of Curriculum Matters papers designed to stimulate discussion about the curriculum as a whole and its component parts. In some cases readers' responses to these papers have also been published. The details of the series titles are shown at the end of this publication.

Classics from 5 to 16, the twelfth in the series, sets out a framework within which schools might develop a programme for the teaching and learning of classics and for the use of classical themes and ideas within the curriculum as a whole. It focuses on the aims and objectives of classics in primary and secondary schools. It considers the implications of these aims and objectives for the choice of content, for teaching approaches, for curricular organisation and for the assessment of pupils' progress.

This paper is addressed not only to heads and teachers but also to school governors, local education authority (LEA) elected members and officers, parents, employers and the wider community outside the school. Like earlier publications in the Curriculum Matters series, this is a discussion paper intended to stimulate a professional debate and to contribute to reaching national agreement about the objectives and content of the school curriculum.

That debate will now take place within the arrangements for developing the National Curriculum contained in the Education Reform Act. It will need to consider not only the use that can be made of the classical world in teaching the prescribed subjects of the National Curriculum but also the claims of classics, as a subject in its own right, to a share of the time available for 'non-foundation' subjects.

This document should be read as a whole, since all sections are interrelated. For example, the lists of objectives must be seen in relation to the defined aims and to what is said about the principles of teaching and assessment.

If you have any comments, please send them to HM Inspector (Classics), Department of Education and Science, York Road, London SE1 7PH, by 30 April 1989.

Introduction

1. Most pupils, both in primary and in secondary schools, encounter material from the Greek and Roman worlds. A smaller number have the opportunity, often in the early secondary years, to take a 'foundation course' in classical civilisation; some have the chance to learn Latin or Greek; and Latin, Greek and classical civilisation are among the subjects which they may choose to study at the GCSE stage and beyond. Although classics no longer holds the place which it once did in the school curriculum, the purpose of this document is to suggest that it has a distinctive contribution to make.

2. Although the Education Reform Act 1988 does not designate classics as a foundation subject of the National Curriculum, many secondary schools will nevertheless want to include it in the time available for 'non-foundation' subjects. At primary level much of what is proposed here could be delivered through subjects which are in the foundation. Some elements of classical civilisation could be provided in this way in the early secondary years too, though careful planning would be needed to give any coherence and the possibility of progression. A separate and coherent course, planned in accordance with the needs and abilities of the pupils and taught or informed by a classics specialist, is preferable; for the classical languages a separate allocation of time is essential.

3. In what follows, two groups of questions are explored:

●   what contact with the classical world is it appropriate to provide for all pupils, and what benefits might they be expected to derive from it?

●   what, in addition, is it reasonable to expect of those pupils whose study of a classical subject has been more extensive or more specialised?

It is hoped that discussion of these issues will be of interest not only to specialist teachers of classics but to other secondary school teachers and to teachers in primary and middle schools, as well as to heads, LEAs, school governors, parents, employers and the wider community.

The nature and scope of the subject

4.   Classics in schools is not confined to the learning of **Latin** and **Greek**. The subject now includes, as well as the classical languages, **'classical civilisation'** – the study of the Greco-Roman world as a whole: its literature and history, its social and political development, its philosophy, art, architecture and technology. The field is vast, and a selection must be made. But whatever the approach and whatever the age of the pupils there are two main reasons for studying the classical world: its intrinsic interest, and its capacity to increase pupils' understanding of themselves and of the world in which they live.

5.   The study of a **classical language,** where it is possible, can add greatly to pupils' knowledge and understanding of the ancient world. A priority in any Latin or Greek course should be to equip pupils to read some classical literature in the original language and hence to gain a deeper insight into the Greeks and Romans – their ways of thought and expression, their attitudes and values – than they might otherwise achieve. Because it is concerned by this means to give pupils a richer appreciation of their own society and culture, a Latin or Greek course is not just a 'language' study. Like any other classical course, it can be seen as a significant contributor to the school's work in the human and social area of experience.

Intrinsic worth

6.   The cultures of Greece and Rome were marked by outstanding achievements in art, architecture, literature, drama, technology, and historical, political and philosophical thought. Any classical course should introduce pupils to a selection of these acknowledged masterpieces as items worth studying in their own right.

Coherence and integration

7.   A distinctive merit of classics, whether approached through a classical language or through artefacts and translated material, is that it deals with periods and cultures in which political, intellectual, literary and artistic developments, and the interaction between them, are often well documented; and which are on a small enough scale to be viewed as a whole. In using classical material, a good teacher

will cross the traditional subject boundaries. In the secondary school, for example, pupils could take a limited span of time and place (such as Athens in the fifth century BC or Rome in the first century AD) and within this begin to build up a coherent picture embracing many different aspects of human experience and achievement.

A common heritage

8. Greece and Rome have also profoundly affected later developments in all these fields both in Britain and elsewhere. The influence of ancient myth – Orpheus, Oedipus, Antigone, Odysseus – has been particularly powerful. Whether pupils are looking at Victorian buildings, comparing democracy with communism, investigating the way their own language works or performing Shakespeare, their understanding can be informed and enriched by familiarity with the general classical background and with the specific allusions which are made. Since much of this cultural and linguistic heritage is shared by otherwise diverse and even antagonistic nations of the modern world, classics offers a useful perspective from which to develop a European awareness and to approach some aspects of multi-cultural education.

A different world

9. The ancient world, in its language and thought, is as profoundly different from our own as it is in some respects strikingly similar. To understand it, pupils must develop an open and sympathetic attitude to the past and the unfamiliar, which in turn should help them to reassess the language, culture and values of the present day and develop a more tolerant attitude to customs and practices unlike their own. Any classical course should develop in pupils a more critical and reflective understanding of the world in which they live.

A powerful stimulus

10. The richness and interest of much (not all) classical material make it readily accessible to pupils of widely differing ages and abilities. In the hands of a skilled teacher it offers an effective medium through which to develop a number of skills and attitudes which most teachers, of any subject, regard as important. For example, whether pupils learn a classical language or not, their contacts with the classical world should kindle their imagination, stimulate an informed personal response and demand rigour and precision – in observation

3

and recording, in the analysis of linguistic features and the abstraction of information, and in the disciplined application of historical judgement.

An understanding of language

11. Any classical course contributes, with other subjects, to pupils' command of their own language. In particular, it can help them to develop a sensitivity to language – especially an awareness of subtlety of expression, shades of meaning, ambiguity and bias. The study of a classical language offers additional opportunities to increase pupils' understanding of their own language and of language in general. Their course will naturally draw attention to the roots of English, Welsh and Romance words, and hence to the underlying richness of their meanings; but it should also focus attention on the means by which ideas are formulated and communicated.

The aims of classics teaching

12. The White Paper 'Better Schools' (1985) suggested that what children learn between the ages of 5 and 16 should help them, among other things, to:

● develop lively, enquiring minds;

● use language effectively;

● develop tolerance of other races, religions and ways of life;

● understand the world in which they live;

● appreciate human achievements and aspirations.

13. The teaching of classical civilisation and classical languages can make a significant contribution to the achievement of these aims. In particular, it should:

● introduce pupils to a selection of the major achievements of the Greeks and Romans in such fields as literature, art, architecture, science, medicine, technology and law;

● introduce pupils to significant aspects of the historical, political and philosophical thought of the classical period;

- kindle their imagination through contact with the classical world and stimulate a personal response;

- develop an open and sympathetic attitude towards the past and the unfamiliar;

- develop a critical and reflective understanding of the world in which they live;

- develop a European awareness through an understanding of their cultural and linguistic heritage;

- develop tolerant but not uncritical attitudes towards customs and practices unlike their own;

- develop pupils' powers of observation, abstraction and analysis of information, judgement and communication;

- enhance their command of language by requiring them to pay close attention to the relationship between concepts and the words and structures used to express them;

- provide an adequate foundation for the study of a classical subject beyond the age of 16.

14.   If the broad aims outlined above are to be implemented in the curriculum, they need to be translated into learning objectives. The following section suggests a range of objectives appropriate to all pupils between the ages of 5 and 14, and to the smaller number who may proceed to a GCSE classical civilisation course. A later section suggests how those objectives may be modified and extended for those who have the opportunity to study Latin or Greek.

Classical civilisation
Objectives in the primary and early secondary years

15.   What pupils learn of the classical world should include elements which make a major contribution to their studies of **language** and **literature**. It should enable them, for example, to:

- increase their understanding of the composition and structure of some English words in common use through an awareness of their classical origins;

- extend their range of vocabulary and give them confidence in handling it;

- develop their appreciation of literature through their contact with writings of different kinds and periods;

- understand some of the purposes, other than literary, for which writing has been used throughout the ages;

- respond imaginatively to what they read;

- improve a range of oral and writing skills.

16. The first two of these objectives are sometimes seen as the preserve of Latin and Greek courses; but an awareness of the classical origins of many English words can begin in the primary school and should be available to all. Children like to know, especially if they are encouraged to work it out for themselves, how *telephone, telescope* and *telegraph* (and such hybrids as *television*) are connected by the idea of distance, or *octagon, octopus, October* and *octave* through their association with the number 8. It can be useful to point out how a simple Anglo-Saxon word can often be matched by one derived from Latin or Greek, which may have added shades of meaning. Examples are: *see, perceive; door, portal; green, verdant.* Drawing attention to words based on the same classical root can help pupils to understand words they have not previously encountered. Exploration of the idea of 'leading' in words with *duct* or *duce* (*conduct, introduce, reduction, seductive*) might prepare the way for some investigation of the force of prepositional prefixes. Some of these aspects of 'language awareness' can be taken much further with pupils who go on to study Latin (see paragraphs 60–61, 66, 74–75).

17. Much Greek and Roman literature can excite the younger reader (stories from the *Iliad* or *Odyssey* of Homer, for instance) or illuminate a topic being studied (for example Caesar's account of the invasion of Britain or Pliny's report of the eruption of Vesuvius). A great deal of 'non-literary' Latin and Greek has also survived and is accessible in translated form: inscriptions from Roman Britain; lettering on Greek vases; recipes from Roman cookbooks; graffiti from Pompeii; inscriptions on tombstones; words on Greek and Roman coins. All these kinds of source-material can put pupils in

contact with what was thought and felt by peoples of other times, while developing their sense of how writing varies in form and expression in accordance with the nature of the audience and the reasons for which it is done.

18.   The telling of Greek and Roman stories (particularly myth and legend) can encourage pupils to respond in a variety of forms including drama, creative writing and other expressive arts. Useful checklists of some oral and written skills which the curriculum should seek to develop in pupils of various ages are to be found in the publication *English from 5 to 16: Curriculum Matters 1*. As that document argues, many of these activities should not be practised in isolation, but should arise in the course of work in various aspects of the curriculum. In this connection, such material as classical myth and legend may have a special contribution to make.

19.   Pupils' learning about the classical world can make an important contribution to the **human** and **social** area of experience. It should enable them, for example, to:

- have direct contact with the material remains of other cultures;

- develop historical concepts relating to chronological sequence, cause and effect, and the nature of evidence;

- become involved imaginatively with the lives of people of other eras and make comparisons between those lives and their own;

- acquire some knowledge and understanding of the sources of their own culture and society;

- develop their own political, moral and spiritual values by comparison with other such values;

- understand something of the functions performed by myth in ancient and modern society.

20.   Like many other periods, the era of the Greeks and Romans may help with the development of certain historical concepts and skills. Materials such as those provided by the extraordinary survival of Pompeii and Herculaneum can be especially potent because of the opportunities they offer to

study ancient historical evidence in great detail. Studying other societies may also help pupils to understand human institutions and to enter through the imagination into aspects of the personal, social and economic lives of others. Pupils' understanding and interpretation of the past, can be helped considerably by visits to local museums and to such sites as Fishbourne, Hadrian's Wall and Caerleon, especially if opportunities can be provided to handle, as well as to look at, artefacts from the Roman world.

21. Exemplars of **moral** judgements and **religious** views drawn from other societies may provide pupils with valuable points of entry into some central questions of human life. Discussion of Greek or Roman attitudes to slavery, the status of women in society, the Olympian gods or gladiatorial contests can help them to articulate fundamental moral questions, discover something of the cultural conditioning on which many of a society's judgements depend, and gain a greater sensitivity to and tolerance of the diversity of values and religious practice in their own world. Listening and responding to myth should be a powerful and enjoyable experience in itself. But many myths point beyond themselves to offer explanations of life and the world and to express society's aspirations, obsessions or fears. In looking at the Greeks' myths of creation or causation, it may be possible to show the extent to which our own world still relies on myths, whether of scientists or of television advertisers.

22. Their experience of the classical world may also help pupils to:

● develop their **aesthetic** appreciation through studying artistic achievements of high quality;

● gain some awareness of the importance of the arts in society;

● develop some of their own **creative** skills;

● understand something of the effects of using different materials and media.

23. Examples may be taken especially from Greek architecture, sculpture and vase-painting, or from Greek or Roman wall-painting, which can give pupils insights into the

development of artistic techniques and opportunities to appreciate the finest expression of those techniques (as in the Parthenon, or the monumental bronze statues from Athens in the fifth century BC). It may be possible to look in a simple way at functional aspects of the arts in the ancient world: the connections between pottery and trade, for example, or between temple or theatre building and the state religious festivals. Pupils may copy or adapt techniques and designs they have encountered, for example in pottery, painting or mosaic-work; and they may be encouraged to respond to stories from myth, legend or history, and to what they have seen at sites and museums, by creating their own dramatic, artistic, musical or literary versions. Ancient societies were restricted in the range of materials, colours and media available to them in their artistic expression and design. It can be valuable to consider how they set about trying to overcome these limitations and to make the most of their natural resources.

24.   Their experience of the classical world may help pupils to:

• understand some basic **mathematical** and **scientific** language and concepts, by comparing ancient and modern practices and attitudes;

• gain some appreciation of the importance of empirical methods in science and technology;

• learn how practical needs can generate **technical** developments;

• develop problem-solving skills by considering practical examples.

25.   Many of the scientific and mathematical achievements of the ancient world are concerned with basic principles from which more complex ideas and hypotheses have subsequently been constructed. Because of this, they can often be appreciated by pupils of primary and early secondary age and give them some notion of the excitement of scientific discovery and the importance of first principles. For example, the principle of the steam engine, atomic theory, the measurement of the earth's circumference and an understanding of the concept of the solar system were all the result of thinking and

9

experiment by individual Greeks. In each case the principles and methods employed can be understood by 11-year-old pupils; and investigation of them can raise important questions about why some of these ideas and discoveries were not built upon or put to practical use in ancient times.

26. Ancient technology provides many possibilities for enabling pupils to exercise skill in reaching solutions to problems. Groups might be invited, for example, to consider the implications of building a new town in Roman Britain using only the range of materials, machinery and techniques on which the Romans depended. Or they might be asked to look at some ancient invention such as the *klepsydra* (water clock) used in Greek and Roman lawcourts, and try to devise a more accurate alternative, using only materials and techniques available in ancient times.

Planning and organisation in the primary and early secondary years

27. In **infant** and **lower junior** classes the pupils' first encounter with the classical world is likely to be through listening to a re-telling of myths and legends, many of which have a direct appeal to young children. They can be a powerful stimulus to the imagination, especially when they involve the supernatural or the fantastic; and they can raise children's awareness of basic questions about morality and truth – 'Was it right to kill the monster?', 'Did it really happen?', 'Could it have happened like that?'. Handling objects from the past and discussing what they are and when they might have been used can help children at this stage to form an idea of chronology – to give a clearer meaning to such expressions as 'long ago' and 'in the olden days'. Objects from the classical world, a piece of broken pottery for example, could be included along with more recent items. Radio and television programmes based on topics from the Greek and Roman world (myth and legend; historical events and famous people; daily life) often elicit worthwhile work in imaginative writing, discussion, dance and drama, painting and model-making. Throughout the infant and early junior years the prime reasons for including classical material in the curriculum must always be its appeal to young children and its capacity to contribute to the aims of primary education. In the process, the seeds may be sown for an interest in, and curiosity about, the classical world which can form the basis of systematic study in later years.

28. In the **upper junior** and **lower secondary** years one principal argument for considering the classical world is its capacity to integrate different aspects of human experience. It is possible to include Greek or Roman components in the planned scheme of work for:

- a major theme (for example water, transport or warfare);

- an individual subject (such as history, geography, English or religious education).

An alternative approach is to focus some of the work on a classical theme which crosses the traditional subject boundaries. A teacher might, for example:

- use a single source from the classical world (a myth, a site-visit, a piece of historical evidence, a passage of literature) as the starting-point for a range of explorations and responses which may embrace many areas of the curriculum;

- make a particular classical period the focus for work in as many areas of the curriculum as possible for a limited period of time (a month or a term, perhaps), so that pupils end this section of their course with a worthwhile insight into the people they are studying;

- select appropriate aspects of the Greco-Roman world as vehicles for achieving specific skills (of observation or communication), attitudes (tolerance, independent thought) or understanding of concepts (for example, cause and effect, slavery, or democracy).

29. In the primary school, any one of these approaches may be planned and implemented either by an individual class teacher or by a small group of teachers sharing their expertise. In the early secondary years many schools find that the kind of 'in-depth' study which is being proposed is most easily organised if 'classical civilisation' can be given its own place in the timetable.

30. Whatever the structural pattern, factual information is not the only, or even the principal, objective. It is far better to explore one myth fully than to learn the factual outlines of 20.

11

Similarly it is more profitable to investigate a single period in some depth than to try to span the whole of Greek and Roman civilisation.

31. At each stage, the **classical content** of the work should be related to the intellectual and emotional development of the pupils and should build on their previous knowledge and experience. For good reasons the topics which pupils encounter in the primary and early secondary years, and the depth to which they study them, will vary from one school to another; they will depend on such factors as the location of the school, the interests and expertise of teachers, and the way the curriculum is organised. However, there are some elements of the classical world which can press a particularly strong case for inclusion in the curriculum because they are:

● readily understood by younger children and available in suitable books;

● intrinsically rich and rewarding;

● able to exemplify and illuminate subjects or themes commonly and appositely treated in these years.

The following paragraphs draw attention to three such elements, each capable of being treated at a variety of levels for pupils of different ages and abilities.

32. **Myth and legend, especially Greek.** Many of the myths and legends from the ancient world are exceedingly vivid, potent and appealing. The case for introducing myth to children is argued forcefully by Elizabeth Cook in *The ordinary and the fabulous*. She writes of the Greek stories:

There is a hard, alert, often cheerful objectivity in the way in which most of them were told in antiquity. It is congenial to children between the ages of 8 and 11 and the best modern versions retain it.

These myths and legends have exerted a powerful hold on the imagination of western Europe and other civilisations ever since, supplying a rich store of images, motifs and stimuli for artists, sculptors, musicians and writers; knowledge of them, therefore, in a sense provides a gateway into the under-standing of much of our cultural tradition. It is impossible to stipulate a precise age at which this material should be introduced. However, of all the sources of classical material encountered by pupils, this should probably be among the first. Not all stories, of course, are equally suitable for younger children, but there is an appropriate nucleus of familiar myths and legends which includes Orpheus and Eurydice; Theseus and the Minotaur; Demeter and Persephone; Atalanta; Zeus and Prometheus; and the legends of Troy.

33. Roman Britain. How strongly the pupils are aware of the Roman remains in Britain may well depend on where they live. Those living near Hadrian's Wall, for example, may well have had an interest in the Romans kindled by visits to some of the principal sites. In other parts of the country, the remoteness of the Romans historically may be matched by the relative inaccessibility of Roman remains. Yet, properly mediated, archaeological sites and artefacts from another period may be an important way of helping to bring a society to life and may pose historical questions in a particularly sharp form. This kind of approach may be especially helpful for pupils aged from 10 to 12, whose chronological perspectives may be hazy but whose curiosity about the past is often great.

34. Roman (and particularly Pompeian) social life. Pupils' contact with some of the physical remains of the culture introduced to Britain by the Romans might lead to a study of aspects of that culture for which the evidence comes from Italy. The extraordinary survival of Pompeii and Herculaneum provides a uniquely graphic source of material with which to illustrate such topics as housing, the family, food and drink, religion and entertainment. Material from this source has been referred to in relation to many of the curricular objectives discussed above, and can form a major component of any classical course for pupils from 12 to 14.

35. To include in the curriculum an agreed selection of classical themes or materials is no guarantee of either a coherent or a progressive experience for pupils: a **planned progression** in the objectives to be achieved is essential. Sometimes, for good reasons, pupils will encounter at 13 or 14 a story, or incident, or topic which they first met at the age of 8. What matters is that the level of response demanded from individual pupils at 13 shall be higher than that which was expected five years earlier; that the objectives to be achieved at each stage shall be carefully planned; and that at each stage

pupils' earlier experiences shall be taken as fully as possible into account.

Objectives in GCSE-related work

36. Many of the objectives identified for the earlier years of the course apply equally to the GCSE stage. They will need to be refined and developed, there will be changes of emphasis, and teaching approaches will naturally incorporate materials of increasing complexity and demand greater maturity of understanding and response; but the framework should still prove useful. In addition, it may be helpful to consider what *The curriculum from 5 to 16: Curriculum Matters 2* terms the elements of learning: the knowledge, concepts, skills and attitudes (and values) which the curriculum seeks to promote.

37. **Knowledge.** Although the acquisition of factual information is not in itself a principal objective of the course, a secure grasp of the evidence which is readily available must always precede, and underlie, the making of judgements and the expression of opinions. What pupils need to know will depend on the particular aspects of the classical world which have been selected for study. Some criteria which might properly influence that selection are set out in paragraphs 42–45.

38. **Conceptual understanding.** A classical civilisation course seeks to use the selected content to impart, through the knowledge which has been acquired, some understanding of a variety of general ideas and concepts – whether literary, philosophical, artistic, political or historical. Many of these concepts take on a distinctive connotation when applied to the classical world. This is true, for example, of such ideas as slave, house, temple, virtue or empire. It can be rewarding to compare the range of meanings which were connoted by the Greek or Roman concepts which correspond most closely to our own words. One specific concept which study of the Greeks (especially) and Romans ought to explore and develop in pupils' minds is antithesis – for example, between human custom and divine law; between theory and practice (or word and deed); between moral duty and expediency, the individual and society, liberty and enslavement.

39. In developing pupils' appreciation of antithesis, the similarities and differences between the classical world and that of today provide many obvious entry-points. Pupils may be helped to recognise that an apparent identity between the classical world and our own may mask important differences. It would be entirely misleading, for example, for pupils to think that only a few peculiarities like the chorus prevent a Greek tragedy from being drama as the twentieth century understands it; or to talk about the fifth-century Athenian popular assembly as if it closely resembled our representative parliament and its citizens conformed to a version of Christian morality. At the same time some superficial differences may conceal essential similarities: many of the political issues which faced the Greeks and Romans are still with us.

40. **Skills** and **capabilities.** The precise intellectual, personal and practical skills developed will vary with the particular topics selected; however, all syllabuses should seek to develop a number of the following skills:

- the capacity, when handling classical material, to observe and record; to abstract and analyse information; to make use of observation to ask questions, solve problems and identify what is relevant to an enquiry; to reason clearly and pay due regard to evidence;

- the ability to respond to the stimulus of the ancient world by using English creatively and critically, and through such practical skills as designing, modelling, painting and acting;

- the capacity to read works of classical literature in translation with enjoyment and understanding, including some appreciation of their literary qualities or historical importance, and some understanding of the author's intentions and technique;

- the development of critical faculties in appreciating products of the visual arts, including architecture, sculpture, painting and pottery;

- the ability to draw on the different aspects of the civilisation studied in order to gain a more coherent picture and perceive inter-relationships; and to use evidence from such sources as archaeological sites and museums to inform this picture.

15

41. **Attitudes** and **values**. A classical civilisation course should be helping to develop such attitudes and values as:

- sensitivity to language, respect for its complexity and awareness of subtlety of expression and shades of meaning;

- readiness to enter into the thought forms, motives and attitudes of widely different cultures;

- respect for reason and the desire to make a well-informed and open-minded approach to problems;

- curiosity about the past, and about the motives and reasons which lie behind human actions;

- receptivity to new experiences and the ideas of other people; a lack of arrogance about our own cultural values;

- developing independence of thought; the growth of personal values and beliefs in religion, morality or politics;

- appreciation of and admiration for the highest qualities in human life and achievement.

Planning and organisation of GCSE-related work

42. The broad aims of a classical course set out in paragraphs 12–14 provide a general framework for the construction of a classical civilisation syllabus for the years leading up to GCSE. They suggest that it should:

- involve the study of items of intrinsic worth and quality;

- promote a coherent view of some aspects of the classical world;

- assist pupils' understanding of the influence of the classical heritage on our own culture;

- enable pupils to explore the contrasts, as well as the similarities, between the classical world and our own;

- exclude material which is unlikely to be accessible and intelligible to pupils of this age;

- contribute to pupils' understanding and use of language by providing opportunities to study, as literature and as evidence, some writing by classical authors.

43. The application of these six principles would have the effect of excluding approaches which, for example, sought to scan the whole classical world from Minoan Crete to the Holy Roman Empire; or which selected three or four unrelated topics almost at random from within this vast compass, or assumed that any item from the classical world was automatically worthy of inclusion.

44. Syllabuses aiming at a coherent, worthwhile experience of the classical world may nevertheless, very reasonably, take many different slants. One syllabus will have a strong historical bias; another may emphasise technology; one will give greater weight to sociological, political or economic aspects and another to literary and aesthetic appreciation. What is important is that the course shall have within it some main focus to which pupils devote a fair proportion of their time and attention. Two periods which have a strong claim to be considered are:

- Greece (especially Athens) in the fifth and fourth centuries BC;

- Rome (and the Roman Empire) in the first century BC and the first century AD.

What marks these two periods out especially is that both witnessed the interaction between social, political, intellectual, literary and artistic developments, and that these movements were fully documented in a variety of ways – with a great deal of the literary and archaeological evidence surviving to this day. Both periods, moreover, were steeped in myth and legend and especially the works of Homer – the *Iliad* and *Odyssey*. These stories may be regarded as the essential backcloth for a properly informed understanding of Greek and Roman civilisation.

45. A classical civilisation syllabus might consist of: (a) all Greek material; (b) all Roman; (c) a Greek section and a

Roman section; (d) topics straddling Greece and Rome. A syllabus which permits candidates to concentrate entirely on one or other civilisation permits greater depth of treatment and closer integration – and, especially if it could be assumed that pupils had studied aspects of the other society in earlier years, this might well be the preferred option. On the other hand, a course containing both Greek and Roman sections invites many fruitful comparisons between the two civilisations – which, in many senses, are not separable. There are attractions in the idea of (d), taking themes (for example the status of women) and considering them in relation to both the Greek and the Roman world.

Principles of teaching and learning

Use of source-material

46.   A classical civilisation syllabus should be firmly based on the evidence provided by the ancient world itself. Primary source-material available to the teacher falls into two broad categories:

● **written** – literary and epigraphic (inscriptions, coinage). There is no shortage of English translations of literary material – some of them extremely daunting in their linguistic and conceptual demands, others readily intelligible to younger or less confident readers. Classical literature is rarely so self-explanatory or straightforward, however, that it can be left for pupils of 14 to 16 to read entirely unaided. Reading aloud in class can be a valuable means of aiding comprehension as well as providing opportunities for discussion of themes and issues raised, or questions of literary appreciation. To juxtapose two or more literary sources, or to set a non-literary item of source material beside the literary evidence, may encourage historical analysis and interpretation.

● **archaeological** – surviving buildings, excavated sites and artefacts (sculpture, painted pottery, functional and decorative objects) housed mainly in museums. Opportunities to exploit archaeological sites or museum visits can be invaluable in adding vividness to pupils' perceptions. Probably nothing can do more to enhance their enjoyment and understanding of the classical world than a properly planned visit to Greece or Italy – a source of learning which is now appreciated and exploited to great advantage by many schools. For much of the work, however, it will be necessary to rely on illustrated books, slides, filmstrips or videotaped materials. They all need to be handled with care; pupils can easily misunderstand the effects of photography – most obviously in the matters of size and scale. Moreover, it can be tempting to accompany the showing of slides and films by over-use of expository teaching methods, and hence lose the opportunity to encourage personal response to what is being shown. One simple – but frequently neglected – way of permitting individual exploration of aspects of classical art is to use hand-held viewers.

Development of independent work

47. Many of the objectives set out above can be realised only if pupils have some scope for working on their own. A frequent method of encouraging such individual work within examination courses at this level is the project, which at its best can yield sustained pieces of personal writing of high quality. It is open to abuse, however. Pupils sometimes have access only to materials which are beyond their level of comprehension; and even where this is not the case there is the risk of wholesale and unthinking copying of text. Some kinds of individual work which may avoid these dangers are:

● independent research which involves analysis of a variety of sources;

● expressive and creative writing or imaginative artwork;

● assignments which exploit pupils' individual skills, such as photography, model-making or computer programming.

A practical focus

48. Classics has sometimes tended to confine itself largely to highly academic, theoretical modes of working, overlooking the great potential of the subject for work of a practical character. To devote time to such areas as the physical and technological can invite attention to practical problems and, if activity is planned accordingly, promote practical skills. One GCSE course, for example, includes a topic on the place of

19

textiles in Greek and Roman society, and provides opportunities for pupils to practise spinning and weaving using the materials and methods employed in the ancient world.

Oral work

49. Undue reliance on written language at the expense of oral work can lead to problems for many pupils in understanding the material which is set before them. It can also restrict their response by not allowing them to articulate their views. Productive talk in class may often occur in a full-class discussion chaired by a teacher; but other groupings may need to be exploited if all pupils are to participate equally in oral work. The possibilities include: pairs debating an issue; small groups talking through a problem they have been set; individual presentations. Classical civilisation courses invite such a variety of treatment – in responding to literature, exploring social or political issues, discussing moral or religious values, interpreting and evaluating visual materials, and performing dramatic sequences (from tragedy or comedy, or based on myth and legend).

Classical languages

Context

50. A language is part of the culture in which it exists; it would be hard to defend a study of the Greek or Latin language which took no account of the ideas, values, culture and achievements of the people who spoke it. It should, as paragraph 11 suggests, foster the development of a variety of logical and linguistic skills. But if it is divorced from its wider context it is likely to become arid and mechanical. If due attention is paid to the broader cultural dimension, then not only is the appeal of the subject widened but it offers richer and more relevant benefits to those who study it. Pupils who begin a Latin or Greek course should therefore be encouraged from the start to see it as a natural extension of whatever work in classical civilisation they have undertaken previously.

51. The Greek and Latin languages are demanding subjects capable of challenging and stimulating the ablest pupils.

Traditionally they were regarded as suitable only for a limited group of pupils at the upper end of the ability-range. Fresh priorities within the subject and new teaching approaches have now brought a classical language within the competence of many more pupils – at any rate in the early stages; but it is reasonable to expect that in most schools the majority of pupils studying Latin or Greek will continue to come from the upper half of the full ability-range.

52.   For a variety of reasons, many of them historical, pupils who have the opportunity of learning a classical language are offered Latin far more commonly than Greek, and most pupils starting Greek already know some Latin. However, the arguments for giving priority to Latin are not overwhelming, and some schools which have a choice might well consider offering Greek first instead. It would follow on naturally from the studies of Greek myth and society which play an important part in many classical foundation courses; the use of an unfamiliar alphabet gives it an immediate appeal to some pupils; and Greek does not suffer from the out-dated prejudices which still affect the attitudes of some pupils, and their parents, towards Latin.

53.   Some pupils who begin a classical language will pursue it to the GCSE stage, or to GCE Advanced level, or may go on to specialise in it at university. Others will not continue beyond the early stages. It is often not possible to predict, when a pupil begins, how far he or she will continue. The teacher of a classical language therefore has to provide pupils with two things:

● a sufficiently firm grounding for subsequent, more specialised study;

● a broad, relevant and coherent experience which is of value in its own right.

This difficult balance is unlikely to be struck unless clear short-term objectives are set up to cover the earlier stages of the course. Without them, the scope of courses is likely to be dominated and narrowed by the requirements of external examinations; and those who do not continue to that stage will experience failure and frustration instead of satisfaction and success.

Objectives in the early stages

The objectives proposed in the following paragraphs, and the examples which illustrate them, are framed in terms of Latin; they should be understood as applying equally, with the obvious minor modifications, to the study of Greek.

Reading

54. The teaching of modern foreign languages at this stage aims principally to develop pupils' ability to communicate in the language. By contrast, a pupil's most direct access to the Romans is through what they wrote, and the principal justification for teaching Latin to the GCSE stage is that it gives direct access to the reading of Latin literature. It is logical therefore that the reading of continuous passages in Latin should occupy a central role from the beginning.

55. What pupils read in the early stages should:

- provide a context in which to acquire, practise and extend an understanding of common grammatical structures;

- be sufficiently interesting in its content to motivate them to explore the meaning and to read further;

- lead them gradually, via made-up or adapted material, towards authentic Latin by introducing them to the 'flavour' of real Latin and to the characteristic literary techniques (vocabulary, word-order, style, tone) of the Roman authors whose works they may later read;

- be set in a context designed to increase their awareness of the society, values and achievements of the Roman world;

- introduce a range of key Roman concepts (such as *familia, servus, civis; dignitas, imperium, virtus*);

- culminate if possible in the reading of some authentic Latin: simple classical texts (a poem of Catullus, or some Ovid, perhaps); inscriptions, including epitaphs and imperial statements (possibly with examples from British churches); ecclesiastical Latin; simple medieval Latin; coinage and mottoes.

56. This reading of authentic Latin is particularly important if there are pupils who will not be proceeding to the later stages of the course; but all should benefit from the realisation, as early as possible, that the Latin they have learnt can be applied to a practical purpose. Many pupils will need considerable help from the teacher, perhaps even the support of an English translation, if they are to explore even the simplest authentic text at this stage; and if time is to be made available for this activity, some other aspects of the work (exploration of some of the more complex grammatical features, for example) may have to be postponed. But the price is worth paying.

Speaking and listening

57. All pupils who have studied Latin, even though not to public examination level, should have:

- listened to good examples of spoken Latin, prose and verse, with accurate pronunciation and expression;

- acquired the skill of speaking passages of Latin aloud confidently, fluently and with reasonable accuracy;

- understood the basic elements of Latin pronunciation, including syllabic length;

- begun to appreciate the importance of the spoken word in Roman society and, especially, the rhetorical character of much literary Latin;

- been introduced to simple examples of such rhetorical devices as alliteration and the use of poetic rhythms;

- gained a practical understanding of the different ways in which emphasis is achieved, in Latin and in spoken and written English.

58. Many pupils begin Latin with the conviction that because Latin is no longer spoken the way it sounded is of little importance. They are likely to be confirmed in their error by teaching approaches which depend heavily on the inspection and analysis of the written word in the text-book or on the blackboard, and regular injunctions to 'look at the Latin', 'find the subject' (or verb, or object) and 'get the

23

words into the right order'. But most Latin literature was designed to be read aloud and to be understood and appreciated aurally, and hearing and speaking the language are important to the learner, for two reasons:

- Because the language is inflected, Latin can modify word-order, more subtly than English can, to shift the emphasis, vary the tone, and convey nuances of meaning. The 'right' order is therefore the Latin word-order, selected by the author as the most effective means of conveying what he has to say; and to grasp the significance of word-order pupils need regularly to hear the language read, and to try reading it for themselves, as well as to see it written down.

- Literary Latin, both prose and verse, depends for much of its effect on the sounds of words, individually and in juxtaposition, and on such rhetorical devices as antithesis and alliteration, which can be fully appreciated only when a passage is read aloud and the words pronounced correctly.

To relegate spoken Latin to the status of an optional extra, to be included if time allows, or to postpone it until the later stages of the course, when 'real' literature can be studied, is seriously to mislead pupils about how the Latin language operates, to ignore some of its most striking characteristics, and to miss important opportunities of comparing and contrasting it with modern English.

Writing

59. What has been said about the reading and speaking of Latin has implications for what pupils write and how they write. Pupils need to respond in writing to the content and feeling of what they read and to be given recognition for their success in this. They should have regular opportunities to:

- express in English, in their own words, the substance of what the Latin is saying – the principal events in the narrative, the main point which the writer is trying to make, or the feeling which the poem conveys;

- experience the satisfaction of translating a passage of Latin into good, clear English, accurately and with due regard to style and tone;

24

- write in good English about the subject-matter of what they have read in Latin and about aspects of the Roman world which they have encountered: this work should include some sustained writing and involve a variety of responses – imaginative, critical, empathetic or analytic.

Learning about language

60. The study of how the Latin language works should aim to enhance pupils' understanding of the nature of English and of language in general. Thus in looking at verbs, for example, and learning about tense, mood and voice, pupils can note common features of Latin and English, distinctive features of each, and the effects of any differences. Provided that they can arise naturally and in context, and be treated without undue abstraction, some complex linguistic concepts can be introduced to pupils, in a simple form, quite early in the course. These might include:

- the different means of conveying tone, emphasis and shades of meaning in English and in an inflected language like Latin;

- the ways of expressing logical relationships in different languages – for example, subject and predicate, negation and the use of conjunction and asyndeton;

- the non-availability of certain forms of expression in one language or the other – for example, the absence of a perfect active participle, generally speaking, in Latin, and the rarity of the subjunctive in English;

- the frequent lack of identity of meaning – untidy overlap rather than precise equivalence – between Latin words and the English words most commonly used to translate them (for example, *taberna*/shop, *iuvenis*/young man, *pati*/suffer, *animus*/mind) and what this tells us about the relative richness of vocabulary in the two languages, the ways in which concepts change over time, and the relationship between 'words' and 'things'.

61. Words of Latin origin greatly enrich the texture of the English language, but they often make it harder to understand. Even a quite elementary knowledge of Latin should extend pupils' ability to infer the meaning of English

words which they encounter for the first time; and it should also help them to incorporate Latinate words into their own active vocabulary. An important aspect of this is to look at the effect of such words on English. Paragraph 74 lists some of the contributions of Latin to English which pupils might be encouraged to identify and discuss at this stage of the course. A comparable list could be devised for Greek.

Objectives at the GCSE stage

62.   The objectives identified for the early years of a Latin or Greek course are intended to draw attention to desirable dimensions of the work; they remain equally valid throughout the years leading to GCSE. In the later stages of the course the pupils' greater maturity and experience of the languages should enable them to improve their understanding and performance in each aspect of the work; move from made-up or adapted material to the original work of Roman or Greek authors; fit what they have learnt of classical language, literature and society into an increasingly coherent pattern; and cope with higher levels of abstraction. But the same strands run through the work; there should be no awkward transition as pupils approach GCSE.

63.   Most pupils who take Latin or Greek in years 4 and 5 will have the GCSE examination as their target – or, if they do not, will work alongside pupils who do; so the teaching must take account of examination requirements. Although the assessment objectives laid down by the national criteria for classical subjects in the GCSE examination are understandably more restricted in scope than the broad range of expectations suggested here for the Latin or Greek course as a whole, there is no conflict between the two. A course designed to implement these suggestions should fully equip pupils for the examination. The following paragraphs take as their starting-point those aspects of the work which are likely to be assessed directly by public examination; but it is assumed throughout that the broad range of objectives already proposed will continue to permeate the course. As before, what is suggested for Latin should be equally applicable to Greek.

The reading of literature

64.   In recent years no more than about 10 per cent of the

pupils who have taken an O-level or GCSE examination in Latin have continued the subject to A-level or beyond. For Greek the figure is around 30 per cent. If a principal purpose of their course is to give them direct access to Greek or Latin literature, this access must be given before the end of year 5; otherwise most are unlikely to put to their intended practical use the linguistic and literary skills which they have acquired. What they read should be authentic Greek or Latin prose or verse literature – and preferably some of each; and it needs to be read 'as literature', not just to provide practice in translation and in the comprehension of grammatical forms and syntactical constructions. Because of limitations of time, pupils may not be able to read complete works at this stage but they should at least read substantial extracts, or anthologies exemplifying some literary genre, not a mere succession of 'unseens' or 'comprehension exercises'. To achieve coherence without undue length it is often appropriate to supplement what pupils read in the original language with passages read rapidly in translation.

65.   Through their reading, pupils at the GCSE stage should have developed the ability (with varying levels of competence and with different amounts of help) to:

- read aloud a passage of Latin or Greek literature with fluency, accuracy and attention to meaning;

- understand what the writer is saying and convey the gist of the meaning in their own words, orally and in writing;

- recognise some of the techniques which the author employs – tone, diction, rhetorical devices, word-order, rhythm;

- express the meaning in idiomatic English;

- appreciate the literary and linguistic qualities of what they have read, both orally and in writing;

- compare the merits of alternative translations.

Competence in the language

66.   Pupils' study of a classical language should by this stage give them the competence and (no less important) the

27

confidence to tackle simple passages of Latin or Greek which they have not met previously; and some understanding of the nature of the Latin and Greek languages and their contribution to English. They should be able, for example, to:

• translate, with the aid of a dictionary where necessary, a short passage of straightforward prose;

• make sense, with the aid of a dictionary and a commentary, of a short passage from an author with whose style they are already familiar;

• use their grasp of syntax to enhance their understanding of nuances of meaning and expression;

• comment on the merits of a proposed translation;

• work out at least the general sense of a simple inscription in a local museum or church;

• apply their knowledge of the language to arrive at the meaning of classically derived expressions which they may encounter in other contexts (such as Latin phrases and abbreviations in common use; words of classical origin found in a modern foreign language which they are studying; brand names of advertised products; ecclesiastical Latin encountered in religious or musical studies; medical and botanical terms; mottoes and coinage);

• recognise specific features of English grammar and vocabulary which owe their origins to Latin or Greek;

• recognise some important differences between Latin or Greek and English (for example, differences of syntax; the influence of inflection; different ways of expressing logical relationships; the frequent lack of a precise equivalence between superficially similar words or concepts); and through this knowledge display an increased awareness of how their own language functions.

67. Pupils who do not go beyond GCSE should find a study of the language which is based on the above priorities both useful and satisfying; and at the same time secure linguistic

foundations will have been laid for further study, not only for those who will proceed directly to an A- or AS-level course but also for those who later on may wish to revive a working knowledge of Latin to support their studies in other fields. For all students the basic expectations are a practical understanding of the main characteristics of the Latin language and the confidence to apply that understanding to the reading of a text.

The classical world

68.   As in the earlier stages, an essential function of a GCSE Latin or Greek course is to enable pupils to have contact at first hand with the lives, thoughts and achievements of the Romans or Greeks; to compare the classical world with their own; and through the discussion of ideas and attitudes prevalent in the ancient world to develop a deeper understanding of important issues of today. The selection of content will be determined to a large extent by the genre and subject-matter of the classical texts which are read; and many of the areas and issues touched on previously can be extended and enriched by the pupils' reading of authentic classical literature. Discussion of political and legal frameworks, for example, may be illuminated by a speech of Cicero; their understanding of Roman attitudes to religion enhanced by a reading of Vergil; and a comparison of ancient and modern attitudes to class, status, wealth and poverty informed by Pliny's correspondence. Where schools find that the linguistic and literary demands of the more usual Latin or Greek course leave too little time for serious treatment of the broader aspects of the classical world, a combined course leading to an examination in Latin and Roman Civilisation or Greek and Greek Civilisation may offer a useful alternative. Such courses retain the full range of objectives of a Latin or Greek course whilst reducing the linguistic and literary content, and thus make more time available for other aspects of the classical world to be studied in some depth.

Principles of teaching and learning

Reading

69.   From the earliest stages pupils benefit from a variety of approaches. Sometimes the class reads a passage together, with the teacher eliciting contributions from everyone; at

other times pupils work in pairs or small groups. They also need regular opportunities, in class or at home, to read and try to understand (but not necessarily translate) a piece of Latin on their own, using dictionaries and grammar-books if they need them. This is important if they are gradually to acquire the self-confidence to apply in practice the linguistic and literary knowledge and skills which they have been taught. Nor is every piece of Latin read for the same purposes. Sometimes, though not too often, a passage is used principally to give practice in handling a particular linguistic feature which recurs in it; sometimes it is read rapidly (and not every sentence is formally translated) for general comprehension; at other times the aim is to produce as accurate and polished a translation as possible, reflecting every nuance of the Latin.

70.   Whatever the focus of a particular lesson may be, it should always be made clear to pupils that:

- they learn Latin grammar in order to read Latin, and not vice versa;

- to comprehend and express the writer's meaning and intention is more important than to reflect precisely the grammatical structures through which he conveys them;

- the subject matter is important, for what it tells them about the classical world and for the light which it may shed on their own;

- an important aim of the course is an increased facility and flexibility in the comprehension and use of English.

71.   It is important not to squeeze artificially into a Latinate mould of grammar those features of English which do not naturally lend themselves to such a treatment. Indeed an aim of the teacher in any such discussion should be to demonstrate the dynamic, evolutionary character of language. Where possible, the pupils' knowledge of other foreign languages should be allowed to contribute further insights, and it may be useful to draw analogies with artificial languages such as BASIC.

Oral work

72.   Not only is it important for pupils to hear Latin spoken and to speak it themselves. Discussion in their own language,

whether in small groups or in a class lesson, is a more effective medium than the written exercise for allowing pupils to contribute their own ideas and suggestions, hear those of others, including the teacher, and weigh up the merits of the various alternatives. Such discussion is essential, from the earliest stages, if pupils are to develop any real grasp of how the Latin language works; through this to gain a better understanding of their own language and of language in general; and in particular to become aware that:

- there is often no neat match of a Latin word to an English equivalent;

- Latin and English have their own natural, and less natural, patterns of syntax. To represent the meaning of a Latin sentence it is not necessary, and is sometimes positively unhelpful, to reflect precisely in English the grammatical structure of the Latin;

- although some suggested translations of a Latin passage can properly be rejected as wrong, there is rarely just a single 'right' translation. Discussion of the alternatives should gradually lead pupils to an awareness of the different criteria by which a translation may be judged.

Writing Latin

73.   Whether pupils at this stage should be expected also to compose in Latin or Greek is an issue on which good teachers differ, sometimes passionately. It is not resolved by discussion of the merits of continuous Latin prose composition as an activity for able sixth-formers and undergraduates. For beginners, some writing of Latin can be useful if it reinforces their grasp of linguistic structures, increases their confidence in handling the language, and hence improves their capacity ultimately to read authentic Latin with understanding and enjoyment. It is not an end in itself. Activities which may give a wider range of pupils the satisfaction of communicating successfully in Latin include:

- completing a Latin sentence by selecting the correct alternative;

- modifying Latin sentences in specified ways;

- constructing their own passages by combining appropriate words from a list provided;

- supplying captions for cartoons, or headlines for stories;

- producing simple inscriptions to a set formula.

Learning about language

74. Learning Latin or Greek should help pupils in their understanding and use of English – by focusing attention on such structural features as syntax, inflection and word-order; by drawing attention to the idea that each word has its distinctive 'area of meaning' and is seldom completely interchangeable with another word, whether in the same language or in a different one; and, most obviously, by enriching pupils' understanding of English words formed, directly or indirectly, from Latin or Greek roots. Work on derivations can easily be seen by pupils as an arid exercise, especially if the English words whose ancestry they are invited to examine are words which they have never used. If the activity is to be seen as having a real purpose, pupils should be encouraged to think, for example, about the **effects** of classically derived words on English; and as far as possible they should do so through discussions which arise naturally in their reading of Latin or Greek. They might be helped to understand, for example, that words of classical origin are used in English:

- to parallel more 'basic' words – verbs especially, but also nouns and adjectives – and that their use often gives the diction a more elevated and poetic (or more artificial and archaic) tone: *prayer/intercession*; *walk/perambulate*; *tearful/lachrymose*;

- to expand ranges of possible meanings where, for certain purposes, 'ordinary' language is insufficiently subtle or discriminating: for example, *gifts/offerings/oblations*;

- to allow abstraction and generate high-level language – for technical discourse in academic disciplines, for instance;

- to provide etymologically intelligible (and sometimes unintelligible) terms for new ideas and objects – often introduced simultaneously into other modern languages;

- to generate clusters of words from the same root but with different prefixes and suffixes: *ducal/duct/ductile*; *reduce/deduce/introduce*; *conduct/aqueduct/viaduct*; *produce/product/production/productive*.

75. Two other aspects of the linguistic heritage of Latin and Greek are worth introducing in the course of pupils' reading of these languages:

- the Latin origins of English vocabulary often, though not always, determine and explain the spelling: for example, *distant* but *persistent*; *desiccate* but *associate*;

- patterns of word-formation can be identified which link English and the Romance languages with Latin and with each other: for example, *-itas* (Latin), *-idad* (Spanish), *-ità* (Italian), *-ité* (French), *-ity* (English). In spite of changes, a lot of basic vocabulary in Spanish, Italian and modern Greek clearly shows its classical origins and may already have been seen by some pupils, especially if they have been on Mediterranean holidays.

Differentiation

76. The Latin and Greek languages are demanding subjects, once reserved for an intellectual élite. Newer teaching approaches, however, have brought them within reach of a much wider range of pupils, and there are teachers who have successfully introduced pupils from virtually the whole ability-range to the early stages of a Latin course. There is no reason why pupils of less-than-average ability should not benefit from some contact with the more elementary aspects of Latin or Greek. As a broad generalisation, however, Latin and Greek are unlikely to be studied with profit *as GCSE examination subjects* by many pupils outside, say, the upper third of the full ability-range.

77. In some schools the corollary of this is that 'classical civilisation', or 'classical studies', has become a subject confined to the average and the less able, or at any rate to those judged unlikely to do well in Latin or, occasionally, a second modern language. Such a hierarchical view is unjustified, and there is no reason why a classical civilisation course should not fully extend the most able.

78. A third type of classical course has gained increasing acceptance in recent years – the 'combined subject' in which Latin and Roman Civilisation (or Greek and Greek Civilisation) carry roughly equal weight. Such an approach can be an effective way of securing, for relatively able pupils, the best of both worlds: knowledge of a classical language and experience of some of its literature at first hand, supported by more extensive reading of literature in translation and the study of other selected aspects of the classical world. A course of this kind should not be regarded as a soft option, and certainly not as an escape-route for pupils who cannot cope with 'real' Latin or Greek.

Classical civilisation

79. In the primary and early secondary years it is neither necessary nor desirable to deprive slow learners of the chance to study material from the classical world or to give the ablest pupils work unrelated to what the remainder of the class are doing. Children of all abilities can enjoy the story of the Cyclops, or benefit from some understanding of the nature of slavery in the ancient world. Differentiation is best achieved through the use of appropriate resources and through variation in the complexity of the tasks set and in the levels of skill required to accomplish them.

80. There are now available many versions of ancient myths and legends at different levels of linguistic demand, both in printed form and on tape. While one pupil may need a shortened version in simplified language and widely-spaced print, another may be quite capable of reading a standard modern translation of the whole of the *Odyssey* or *Iliad*. Similarly, while simplified histories of aspects of the ancient world will be sufficient for many pupils, some can and should handle more detailed and more demanding books. All pupils should have some acquaintance with primary sources and materials. But some materials will be more suitable for the more able: Seneca's essay on slavery, for example, in which he reflects that slaves are human beings, not chattels, might be stimulating and thought-provoking for some pupils of 11 or 12.

81. Pupils of different abilities can cope with different levels of complexity and abstraction. At one level, the Cyclops story presents a simple and exciting account of the outwitting of an

evil monster. At another, it presents in stark focus some very distinct and, by modern standards, startling values and customs. Why, for example, does the author find it quite acceptable for Odysseus to consider stealing Polyphemus' goats and sheep? The custom of exchanging gifts focuses attention on the relationship of myths to the historical realities which lie behind them. There is an obvious similarity between this story and others – some, like 'Sinbad the Sailor', influenced by it, others apparently independent. These are not graded alternatives, nor do they exhaust the possibilities of this theme. They are intended only to suggest that what for some pupils is no more than a straightforward adventure-story can enrich the experience of others by challenging their understanding and powers of analysis to their full capacity.

82.   In the two years leading up to the GCSE examination, a class is likely to contain pupils of widely different interests and abilities. To some extent these can be accommodated by the selection of different options both for the written examination and for internally assessed coursework. One group, for example, might concentrate on the philosophical ideas in Plato's *Apology* while another worked on aspects of art and architecture. Where a class is divided in this way, the balance between individual working and group activity, with or without the direct involvement of the teacher, needs to be watched carefully. If a prescribed examination syllabus contains a large measure of common content, differentiation may need to be achieved by setting pupils different tasks on the same material, as was suggested earlier for the Cyclops story. One essential aspect of differentiation in day-to-day classwork is sensitivity to the pitch of the lesson and the demands of the language used, whether the teacher's or from the text-book. For some pupils Greek and Roman terminology and names can prove a barrier because of their length and unfamiliarity.

Classical languages

83.   Differentiation in the teaching of a language poses the problem common to all subjects in which development is 'linear': some pupils master the essential skills at a faster rate than others. If the work of the class proceeds at a uniform pace the more able become bored or the less able bewildered. Yet to allow pupils to work through the same material at their own pace is likely to open up such great gaps between them that

even the best teacher cannot supply the unflagging individual attention which is required; it also rules out the possibility of having a group of pupils, or the whole class, discussing together the meaning or translation of a passage of Latin or Greek.

84. A more promising approach is to let pupils move at the same pace through the basic material of the course, but to limit or extend the demands made on individual pupils at each stage. Some may be asked to produce a polished translation while others simply give an outline of the story they have read. Some may read a passage without access to the vocabularies or grammar-notes which others may need. An able pupil may be given the chance to supplement the basic reading-material of the course by reading and responding to some passages of authentic Latin or Greek at an earlier stage than the rest of the class.

85. Differentiation is not just a matter of meeting the needs of more-able and less-able pupils. Learning Latin or Greek involves a wide range of skills, and pupils who are highly competent in one may be relatively weak in another. For example, a pupil who finds little difficulty with the analysis of linguistic structures (traditionally the accepted measure of competence in a classical language) may be far less good than others in the group at responding to literary questions or coping with the social, political or historical context. For a pupil who has made rapid progress in one of these areas, enrichment may consist in strengthening his or her competence in another.

Assessment

86. Some of the main purposes of the assessment of pupils are listed in *The curriculum from 5 to 16: Curriculum Matters 2.* They are to help teachers:

- to diagnose individual pupils' strengths and weaknesses;

- to match the work of the classroom to their capabilities;

- to guide them into appropriate courses and groups;

- to involve them in discussion and self-appraisal;

- to inform parents of the pupils' progress;

- to see how far planned objectives are being fulfilled, for individual pupils and for the class as a whole;

- to adjust objectives and teaching approaches accordingly.

These purposes require a clear definition of expectations (as expressed through the aims and objectives of the subject and through the scheme of work); effective methods of assessment in the classroom day by day; and procedures for recording and reporting progress which can be used and understood by others. A fourth requirement, at the secondary level, is less immediately within the control of the individual school: a system of external examinations which supports the curriculum without distorting it positively encourages teaching approaches that are educationally desirable, and complements the school's internal patterns of assessment.

87.   The identification of reasonable expectations is an essential first stage. In most primary schools and in the early years of some secondary schools (for example, where classics forms part of a combined humanities programme) objectives for the teaching of classics are unlikely to be listed separately but will be subsumed under other areas of the curriculum. For classics courses elsewhere, the earlier chapters of this document suggest a number of possible frameworks (areas of learning and experience; knowledge, concepts, skills and attitudes; listening and speaking, reading, writing and understanding of language and cultural context). No such framework is entirely satisfactory: schools will properly decide for themselves how best to organise the list of expectations which they produce, and may indeed feel that different classical courses are best served by different kinds of framework. What is essential is that the expectations identified and the degree of emphasis accorded to each should genuinely reflect what the pupils are to spend their time doing and what the course as a whole is intended to achieve. A checklist of expectations should not (as can easily happen) be a programme of desirable extras which omits – because it takes for granted – the teacher's real priorities.

88.   The various objectives of the course will not, usually, be served in isolation, by separate items of work: such an approach would so itemise the pupil's learning that coherence

would inevitably be lost. A more useful approach may be to construct a 'grid', with items of work on one axis and objectives (with an indication of their relative importance) on the other, so that:

- for any one item of work, the teacher is conscious of the objectives to which it will contribute, and the degree of emphasis to be attached to each; and

- over a period of time, each objective can receive its due share of attention.

89. Such a grid can be developed further, to serve as an instrument for the informal assessment of the individual pupil's progress, so that as the year proceeds the teacher builds up not just a succession of scores for the different items of work but a profile of the pupil's success in meeting each of the principal expectations of the course. For this to be possible:

- global 'marks' and general comments need to be replaced (or at least supplemented) by more detailed assessments which draw attention to particular strengths and weaknesses; and

- the full range of principal expectations needs to be assessed in a balanced way – not just those which can most easily be measured objectively and reduced to numerical terms.

Assessment of the kind suggested here will be diagnostic and formative, not merely summative; and it will take account of all aspects of a pupil's performance, affective as well as cognitive, oral as well as written. It is likely to be, for the most part, subjective and impressionistic, but this is unavoidable if it is to cover the full range of expectations.

90. In Latin teaching, increasing interest is being taken in the use of graded tests of attainment closely related to particular coursebooks in common use, with national certification. Those already in operation helpfully focus attention on aspects of the subject which can easily be neglected – for example, perception of the sense of a Latin passage (as distinct from the production of a translation),

awareness of the social and historical context, and spoken Latin. Moreover, since any pupil who has been well taught and has worked with reasonable application should be able to gain a high mark, they may be expected to motivate pupils by providing an assurance that measurable progress has been made.

Conclusion

91.   Classics in some form is taught in between a quarter and a third of maintained secondary schools and in the majority of independent schools; some use of themes and materials from the classical world is made in many primary schools too. In recent years new approaches to the study of both the classical languages and other aspects of the classical world have prompted a reconsideration of the purposes which classics can serve, enlivened the teaching and aroused the enthusiasm of pupils. The aim of this document has been to show how the study of classics can contribute to the education of pupils of all ages and abilities.

Printed in the United Kingdom for Her Majesty's Stationery Office
Dd. 8053499   11/88   C65

Curriculum Matters:
an HMI series

Titles already published are:

1. *English from 5 to 16* second edition incorporating responses. HMSO, 1986, £2.50
   ISBN 0 11 270595 2
2. *The curriculum from 5 to 16* HMSO, 1985, £2.00
   ISBN 0 11 270568 5
3. *Mathematics from 5 to 16* second edition incorporating responses. HMSO, 1987, £2.95
   ISBN 0 11 270616 9
4. *Music from 5 to 16* HMSO, 1985, £1.50
   ISBN 0 11 270579 0
5. *Home economics from 5 to 16* HMSO, 1985, £2.00
   ISBN 0 11 270580 4
6. *Health education from 5 to 16* HMSO, 1986, £2.00
   ISBN 0 11 270592 8
7. *Geography from 5 to 16* HMSO, 1986, £2.50
   ISBN 0 11 270606 1
8. *Modern foreign languages to 16* HMSO, 1987, £2.00
   ISBN 0 11 270612 6
9. *Craft, design and technology from 5 to 16* HMSO, 1987, £2.00
   ISBN 0 11 270642 8
10. *Careers education and guidance from 5 to 16* HMSO, 1988, £2.00
    ISBN 0 11 2706487
11. *History from 5 to 16* HMSO, 1988, £2.00
    ISBN 0 11 270660 6

English from 5 to 16: The responses to Curriculum Matters 1 HMSO, 1986, free
ISBN 0 85522 195 X

The curriculum from 5 to 16: The responses to Curriculum Matters 2 HMSO, 1988, free
ISBN 0 85522 182 8

Mathematics from 5 to 16: The responses to Curriculum Matters 3 HMSO, 1987, free
ISBN 0 85522 199 2